A Teen's
to Basic Cooking

Gabbie Krivonak

Copyright © 2021 by Gabbie Krivonak

ISBN 978-1-9701-0942-9

Published April 2021

ANEWPRESS

This book is dedicated to
my grandchildren, Drew, Katie, Dan, Khloe, Nick, and Olivia.
Love, Oma

RECOMMENDED DIET FOR TEENS

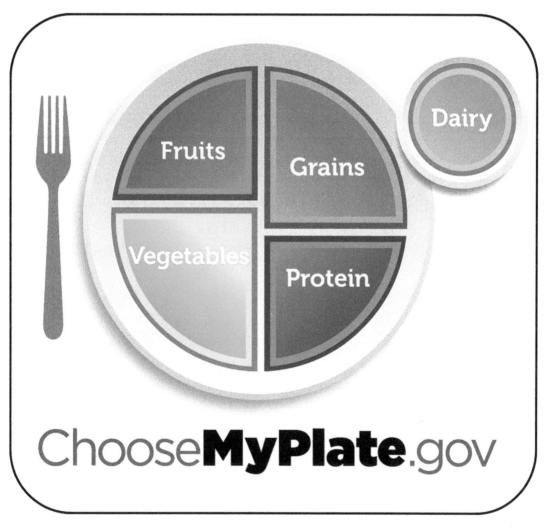

Courtesy of the Department of Agriculture: My Plate

CONTENTS

———

Introduction 9

Required Kitchen Equipment and Supplies 11

Cooking Fundamentals

    The Five Basic Tastes 17
    Basic Knife Skills 21
    Cooking Methods 25
    Use of Herbs and Spices 27
    Basic Food Safety 29
    Reading a Recipe 31
    Measuring 33

Teen-Friendly Recipes

    Vegetables 37
    Potatoes 45
    Entrees 55
    Desserts 85

Cooking Terms 97

Index 103

Introduction

Since my last book was published, I have been teaching teens how to cook in summer camps and after-school classes. I found teenagers really love to cook and it is a skill to carry with them for their entire life. It is even more fun when learning with friends, and the best part is they get to eat what they cook! This book covers the basic skills and safety measures necessary to perform well in the kitchen.

Initially, this book was going to be a manual for teachers of after-school cooking classes. The pandemic changed all that. Not only are schools virtual, but after school sports and classes were cancelled. I thought, "What better thing to do while quarantined than to learn to cook?"

I have divided the book into two sections; a skills section and a teen-friendly recipe section with recipes teens will want to cook and eat. They are simple and do not need complicated equipment or kitchen gadgets. I know that everyone wants teens to eat well for energy and health, but going heavy into kale and things made with twigs and berries is not the place to start. Learn the basics of cooking with recipes teens like; a nutrition class can help them to eat healthy.

I have tried to keep the recipes' ingredients as inexpensive as possible and I have included some global recipes to pique interest in the food of other countries and ethnicities.

Most of all, I want to inspire teens to learn a new skill and enjoy the creativity that comes with cooking a good dish and sharing it with others.

Required Kitchen Equipment and Supplies

As with any craft, cooking requires equipment and tools to complete the process. Most kitchens have the basics. Familiarize yourself with the pots and pans and tools that your kitchen currently possesses. Before making any recipe, check to see if you have all the equipment required. The only thing that you might want to invest in is a good chef's knife. The chef's knife is the basic tool you will use in almost every recipe. Once you have taken inventory and know where each item is located, it will become second nature to reach for the right tool without thinking about it. A variety of bowls of different sizes are required. Stainless steel bowls are preferable.

Equipment like food processors, mixers, blenders and the like can be necessary for certain recipes. If your kitchen doesn't have any of these, keep a lookout for yard sales and the Facebook Marketplace where you can pick tools and equipment for very little money. Otherwise, you can blend and chop by hand with a whisk and a chef's knife.

There are certain basic supplies that a working kitchen needs to have. All-purpose flour, granulated sugar, extra-virgin olive all (sometimes abbreviated as EVOO), and a variety of basic herbs and spices, such as paprika, chili powder, Italian seasoning, garlic, and bay leaf. Be sure to check the herbs and spices required before starting a recipe. Baking requires baking soda, baking powder, and vanilla, at a minimum. Baking also requires special pans for making cakes, cupcakes, and cookies.

Add salt and pepper to the list as well as a full apron. Cooking gets messy and clothes need to be protected. A supply of dish towels, scrubbing sponges and dish detergent will be required for cleanup.

Basic Equipment List

- Stirring spoons (wooden or strong plastic)
- Spatula
- Rubber scraper
- Slotted spoon
- Tongs
- Rolling pin
- Meat mallet
- Stainless steel mixing bowls (various sizes)
- Colander
- Measuring spoons (set)
- Sieves (large and small)
- Pyrex measuring cup (for liquid ingredients)
- Ice cream scoop (for baking)
- Vegetable and fruit peeler
- Chef's knife
- Paring knife
- Kitchen shears
- Cutting boards
- Sheet pans
- Muffin/cupcake pan
- Round cake pans
- Roasting pan
- Instant-read thermometer
- Sauté pan
- Sauce pans
- Dutch oven
- Hand mixer
- Standing mixer
- Food processor
- Blender
- Whisk

See how many tools and what equipment you can find in your kitchen!

Courtesy of Shutterstock

COOKING FUNDAMENTALS

———

I   The Five Basic Tastes
II   Basic Knife Skills
III Cooking Methods
IV Use of Herbs and Spices
V   Basic Food Safety
VI Reading a Recipe
VII Measuring

The Five Basic Tastes

1

THE FIVE BASIC TASTES

———

Learning to cook requires some understanding of the five recognized tastes: sweet, sour, bitter, salty, and umami.

Sweet foods can be found in about 60% of all recipes. It may come as a surprise that sweet foods include whole grains, vegetables, beans, and fruit. These sweet things complement the other tastes. Sweetness signals to the brain that it is about to be fed the energy source it needs to conduct many bodily functions. Sweetness does not mean tons of granulated sugar.

Sour is a taste that is easily recognizable. It is a result of acidity and makes your lips pucker. It is interesting which foods fall into this category; yogurt has a sour flavor, often made more palatable by adding the sweetness of fruit. Lemons, limes, pickles, and salad dressings are sour foods too. Vinegar is also used in some sour-tasting recipes.

Many people shy away from things that are **bitter**. Arugula greens can be bitter and this flavor is found in a lot of leafy greens. One bitter flavor, dark chocolate, makes up for the bitterness of all those other foods.

Salty foods contain some form of sodium chloride, which is a basic health necessity. Every recipe, including baked goods, calls for salt. Salty snacks like potato chips, tortilla chips, and the universal French fries are very popular. Unfortunately, too much salt can lead to high blood pressure and other ailments later in life. These foods can also be empty calories.

The last of the five tastes is **umami**, which means "good flavor" in Japanese. It was only recognized in the early part of the 20th century in Japan, and just since 1985 in Western countries. Umami is an item like soy sauce or MSG (monosodium glutamate). Mushrooms added to a recipe gives an umami taste; it is sometimes called "savory" instead of umami.

One of the reasons understanding basic tastes is important is because as you grow as a chef, these tastes are the foundation for making a dish without a recipe. As you become more proficient, try putting together a dish just from the ingredients in the refrigerator and pantry with no recipe to guide you. It is a lot of fun!

Basic Knife Set

11

BASIC KNIFE SKILLS

———

Using knives properly is a fundamental cooking skill that you should learn early. It is essential to know the types of knives, what each is used for, and how to safely handle them. The following is a list of knives and their function:

Knife Terminology

- **Chef's Knife** — A chef's knife is broad and stiff with a slightly curved blade. The blade is 8 to 13 inches long and up to 3 inches wide. A chef's knife is used mostly for chopping (garlic, onions, fresh herbs, shallots, chocolate, etc.) and for heavy-duty slicing. After much use and sharpening, the edge of a chef's knife may curve inward so that it does not lie flush against a cutting board and its ability to chop finely is limited. At this point, it must be reground or replaced.

- **Paring Knife** — In the shape of a miniature chef's knife, the paring knife is designed for peeling of fruits and vegetables, A crescent-shaped paring knife is used specifically for carving fruits and vegetables.

- **Boning Knife** — A boning knife has a sturdy handle and a narrow, tapered, pointed blade and is designed to separate meat from bones. A stiffer blade is used for deboning meat with larger bones, while more flexible blades are for deboning meat with smaller bones.

- **Slicer** — Slicers are 10 to 14 inches long, $\frac{5}{8}$ to $1\frac{1}{2}$ inches wide, and slightly flexible. Slicers with a tapered point are used for slicing cooked meats with bones; slicers with a rounded end are used for boneless cooked meats.

- **Serrated Slicer** — Blades with a serrated edge are used for slicing crumbly or crusty foods like bread and brioche. Serrated knives are also good for cutting through tough fibrous foods such as fruits and vegetables.

Basic Knife Cuts

- **Coarse Chopping** — Usually used for items that will not be part of the finished dish, such as a mixture of onions, celery, and carrots used to flavor stock

- **Mincing** — A relatively even, very fine cut; especially appropriate for herbs and flavoring agents such as garlic and shallots

- **Long Rectangular Cuts**
  - **Julienne**: A long rectangular cut 1/16 x 1/16 x 1 to 2 inches in length
  - **Batonnet(as in baton)**: A cut ¼ x ¼ x 1 to 2 inches in length

- **Cube Cuts**
  - **Small Dice**: A ¼ x ¼ x ¼ inch cut
  - **Medium Dice**: A ⅓ x ⅓ x ⅓ inch cut
  - **Large Dice**: A ¾ x ¾ x ¾ inch cut

- **Other Cuts**
  - **Rondelle**: A simple cut used for cylindrical vegetables such as carrots or parsnips, which produces a round disk. May be varied by cutting on the bias (diagonal)
  - **Oblique or Roll Cut**: Used primarily on cylindrical vegetables. The peeled vegetables are cut on the diagonal then rolled 180° (a half turn) and cut through on the same diagonal
  - **Chiffonade**: Also known as a ribbon cut, it is used to efficiently cut leafy vegetables and herbs into finely sliced strips or ribbons

Knife Safety

- Keep your blades sharp!

- Only cut on appropriate surfaces—never on metal, glass, or hard stone such as marble or granite.

- Never attempt to catch a falling knife.

- Use the right knife for the task at hand.

- Never use a knife for any purpose other than what it was intended (never use your knife to open a can or pry something loose).

- Do not leave your knives in a sink full of water.

- Pass a knife by its handle.

- Always cut away from yourself; never cut toward yourself.

- Hold your knife by gripping the handle with your fist.

- Keep fingers on your guiding hand curled.

- When walking with a knife, hold it close to your side with the tip down and the blade facing away from you.

III

COOKING METHODS

———

Picking the right cooking method and understanding the terminology that describes it is an important cooking skill. When someone cannot cook at all, it is often said they "can't even boil water." Knowing how to boil and poach (not to mention roast, bake, sauté, and broil) are the foundations of cooking.

Boiling requires the temperature to reach 212°F (100°C). Boiling is indicated by large bubbles rising to the surface and the production of steam. When something is at a rolling boil, the bubbles are continuously forming at the top of the liquid. Boiling is a technique that is used for boiled eggs and pasta.

Simmering means that a few small bubbles rise to the surface every two or three seconds. Simmering occurs between 185°-200°F (29°-38°C). Simmering is used in making sauces and soups.

The ability to master the two techniques above is in controlling the heat and recognizing the signs of boiling and simmering. For example, when poaching an item like eggs or fish, the entire item must be submerged in the simmering liquid.

Roasting and **baking** are techniques for beef, pork roasts, cakes, and cookies, among many other examples. The essence of this method is to cook a dish uncovered in an oven. Heat is transferred from the outside of the food to the inside. This type of cooking takes time; it is important to check the temperature of a roast by inserting a thermometer into the center of the meat. It is also why you test the doneness of a baked good by inserting a tester into the middle of it.

One technique to use when roasting meat is to sear and bake. I learned this in cooking school and use it all the time. You take a roast and **sear** it over very high heat to form the savory crust on the meat. You can then bake the meat in an oven either immediately or at a later time. This gives you great flexibility if you are cooking for guests.

The word **sauté** is a French term that comes from "sauter" which means to jump. This describes the action of the food when tossed into a hot pan. Of course, this aptly describes a TV chef tossing his ingredients into the air from his/her sauté pan.

Sautéing requires a very hot pan, cooking oil, and ingredients dusted with flour or patted dry before sautéing. The pan must be preheated and the food is cooked at high heat. When the food is removed from the pan, the pan is often deglazed. This means adding wine or another compatible liquid to the hot pan and dissolving the brown bits of food left in the pan. This deglazed mixture is often used to make yummy sauces to accompany the dish.

Another concept associated with roasting and sautéing is called **resting**. This means allowing the meat to sit for 10 to 15 minutes, during which time it continues to cook internally and absorbs juices for a moist taste.

Broiling is the use of radiant heat from above. This can be used for meat or for browning the tops of dishes like lasagna or mac and cheese.

There are more cooking methods and techniques in the glossary.

IV

USE OF HERBS AND SPICES

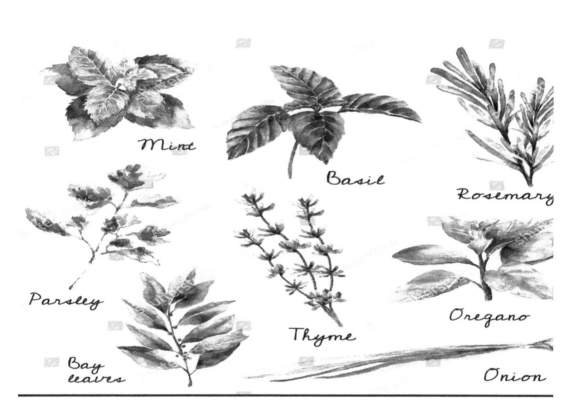

Mint

Basil

Rosemary

Parsley

Thyme

Oregano

Bay leaves

Onion

Using herbs and spices in cooking is extremely important; otherwise, dishes will lack taste. Different styles of cooking are usually defined by the blend of herbs and spices. Italian cooking is known for the use of basil, oregano, and garlic. Mexican food uses cilantro and cumin. Having a wide selection of herbs and spices on hand is pretty basic. They can be expensive, though. If you have the outdoor space, you can grow many herbs in containers on a back porch and even on a kitchen window sill. Fresh herbs are almost always better than dried herbs, but are not always available. A variety of dried herbs certainly work when it is not possible to obtain fresh. Look for dried herbs in any grocery store. They are frequently on sale two for the price of one at Safeway. Store brands are always cheaper than brand names. Costco and Sam's Club have good prices.

V

Basic Food Safety

- Wash hands thoroughly with soap and warm water for at least 20 seconds and dry with a paper towel or clean cloth.

- Keep cold foods cold and hot foods hot until it is time to eat them.

- Do NOT cross contaminate! Use one cutting board and knife for meats and another cutting board and knife for fresh produce.

- Wash hands immediately after handling raw meat, poultry, and fish.

- Cook to a safe temperature. Refrigerate leftovers promptly.

- Wash and scrub fresh fruits and vegetables before use.

- Use equipment in a safe manner.

You should have a small first aid kit available. They are not too expensive and can come in handy for small cuts or burns.

Safe Minimum Cooking Temperatures

The chart below shows the minimum temperature each category of food must achieve to be considered safe to eat.

Category	Food	Temperature °F	Rest Time
Ground Meat & Mixtures	Beef, pork, veal, lamb	160	None
	Turkey, chicken	165	None
Fresh Beef, Veal, Lamb	Steaks, roasts, chops	145	3 minutes
Poultry	Chicken & turkey, whole	165	None
	Poultry breasts, roasts	165	None
	Poultry thighs, legs, wings	165	None
	Duck & goose	165	None
	Stuffing (cooked alone or in the bird)	165	None
Pork & Ham	Fresh pork	145	3 minutes
	Fresh ham (raw)	145	3 minutes
	Precooked ham (to reheat)	140	None
Eggs & Egg Dishes	Eggs	Cook until firm yolk	None
	Egg dishes	160	None
Leftovers & Casseroles	Leftovers	165	None
	Casseroles	165	None
Seafood	Fin fish	145 (or flesh is opaque)	None
	Shrimp, lobster, and crabs	Flesh is pearly and opaque	None
	Clams, oysters, and mussels	Shells open during cooking	None

VI

READING A RECIPE

———

It is something cooking teachers must say 1,000 times: "Read the recipe." I had a colleague who answered each question her students asked her by saying, "Did you read the recipe?" It is probably why the famous chef Julia Child said, "If you can read, you can cook."

If you don't read the recipe completely, you may find that you have made some fatal mistake that makes the dish a disaster. Everyone has done it. You use all of an ingredient in the beginning and then find half of the ingredient should have been saved for step 10.

Make sure you read through the recipe at least twice, understand it, and can perform the techniques required. Assemble all of the ingredients, tools, and equipment at your cooking station. This is called *mis en place* from the French, meaning "put in place."

Understand how many servings the recipe makes and decide whether it should be halved, quartered, or even doubled to feed a whole group. This is when all the fractions you learned in elementary school become very useful. Remember to preheat the oven if the recipe requires it.

The term *divided* in a recipe such as "½ cup and 2 tablespoons of butter, divided" means that you do not use all the butter at the beginning of the recipe; you need the two tablespoons of butter near the end of the recipe.

If you don't understand some instruction in a recipe, google the technique or search for a video on YouTube that demonstrates it.

In recent times, the Food Channel and TV shows like Iron Chef along with celebrity chefs like Rachel Ray and Bobbie Flay have stimulated a new interest in cooking and food in general. You can stream these shows and watch other chefs on TV as well.

VII

MEASURING

The importance of accurately measuring ingredients cannot be stressed enough. Good measuring can make or break a dish. Here is another time you can apply all your math knowledge to a practical activity.

The first order of business is to have an accurate set of measuring cups, measuring spoons, and thermometers. The following equipment is also needed:

- Liquid measuring cup, like a 2-cup glass Pyrex

- Dry ingredient measuring cups from ¼ to 1 cup

- Measuring spoons from ⅛ teaspoon to 1 tablespoon

- Instant-read thermometer

- Oven thermometer

- Timers

Proper measuring is essential in baking. Dry ingredients must be leveled at the top using a knife or small spatula. Liquid measurements cannot be measured in dry measuring cups because they cannot be filled to the very top as required because of spillage. This concept seems is hard to grasp for many entry-level cooks.

Weights and Measurements

Cooking weights and measures are used every day in culinary school. Here is a table showing equivalences between some common units of measurement to help you convert between them.

US Liquid Measurements and Dry Measurement

Unit	Equals	Also Equals	Unit	Equals
1 teaspoon	⅓ tablespoon	⅙ fluid ounce	⅛ teaspoon	A pinch
1 tablespoon	3 teaspoons	½ fluid ounce	3 teaspoons	1 tablespoon
⅛ cup	2 tablespoons	1 fluid ounce	⅛ cup	2 tablespoons
¼ cup	4 tablespoons	2 fluid ounces	¼ cup	4 tablespoons
⅓ cup	¼ cup + 4 teaspoons	2 ¾ fluid ounces	⅓ cup	5 tablespoons
½ cup	8 tablespoons	4 fluid ounces	½ cup	8 tablespoons
1 cup	½ pint	8 fluid ounces	¾ cup	12 tablespoons
1 pint	2 cups	16 fluid ounces	1 cup	16 tablespoons
1 quart	4 cups	32 fluid ounces	2 cups	16 ounces
1 gallon	4 quarts	16 cups	1 pound	16 ounces

Temperature Definitions		Oven Heats	
Simmering point of water	180°F	Very Slow to Slow	250°-300°F
Boiling point of water	212°F	Moderately Slow	325°F
Soft-ball stage for syrups	234°-240°F	Moderate	350°F
Hard-crack stage for syrups	290°-310°F	Moderately Hot	375°F
Caramel stage for syrups	320°F	Hot to Very Hot	400°-500°F

TEEN FRIENDLY RECIPIES

Bologna Italy

VEGETABLES

———

Roasted Green Beans with Parmesan & Basil

INGREDIENTS:

¾ to 1 pound fresh green beans, trimmed
1 tablespoon extra-virgin olive oil
¾ teaspoon dried (or fresh) basil
¼ teaspoon salt
¼ teaspoon freshly cracked pepper (more or less to taste)
2 tablespoons grated Parmesan

PREPARATION:

1. Preheat oven to 425°F (218°C).

2. Dry green beans well and spread on a rimmed baking sheet. Toss with olive oil (use your hands), so that all the beans are coated. Sprinkle with basil, salt, and pepper. Toss again to coat.

3. Roast for 10 minutes, toss, and continue to roast for 5 more minutes. Remove from the oven, immediately sprinkle with Parmesan, and serve.

Note: These would be amazing with fresh instead of dried basil (but they're also amazing as is). If you have fresh basil, don't add before roasting; wait until the green beans are cooked and then toss with the finely minced basil leaves.

Serves 4

Adapted from recipe by Rachel Cooks

Baked Parmesan Zucchini

INGREDIENTS:

Spray cooking oil
½ cup freshly grated Parmesan
½ teaspoon dried thyme
½ teaspoon dried oregano
½ teaspoon dried basil
¼ teaspoon garlic powder
Kosher salt and freshly ground black pepper, to taste
4 zucchinis, quartered lengthwise
2 tablespoons of olive oil
2 tablespoons chopped fresh parsley leaves

PREPARATION:

1. Preheat oven to 350°F (177°C). Coat a baking sheet with nonstick spray and set aside.

2. In a small bowl, combine Parmesan, thyme, oregano, basil, garlic powder, salt and pepper to taste.

3. Place quartered zucchini onto prepared baking sheet. Drizzle with olive oil and sprinkle with Parmesan. Bake until the zucchini is tender, about 15 minutes. Then broil for 2-3 minutes or until crisp and golden brown.

4. Garnished with parsley and serve immediately.

Serves 4

Adapted from DamnDelicious website

Ratatouille

Courtesy of Shutterstock

Ratatouille

INGREDIENTS:

2 tablespoons olive oil
2 cloves garlic, diced
1 onion, sliced
2 small eggplant, peeled and diced
2 small zucchini, peeled and sliced
4 large tomatoes, chopped
2 tablespoons tomato paste
2 teaspoons chopped basil
2 teaspoons flat leaf parsley, diced
½ teaspoon (or more) kosher salt
Fresh ground pepper to taste

PREPARATION:

1. Add olive oil to pan and heat until hot but not smoking. Sauté garlic and onions for about 3 minutes.

2. Add eggplant and sauté for about 2 minutes, then add zucchini and sauté for another 2 minutes.

3. Add chopped tomatoes and tomato paste and bring to a simmer for 5 minutes.

4. Add herbs, salt, and pepper, simmering for another 3 minutes.

5. Remove from heat and serve.

Serves 4

Recipe from My Mom's a Good Cooker website

Mesclun Salad

Courtesy of Shutterstock

Mesclun Spring Mix Salad with Balsamic Vinaigrette

INGREDIENTS:

Salad:
6 ounces (about 4 cups) mesclun spring mix
3 veggies such as cucumbers, cherry tomatoes, or sliced carrots
Several slices of shaved Parmesan

Vinaigrette:
2 tablespoons balsamic vinegar
½ teaspoon Dijon mustard
Pinch of salt
8 tablespoons olive oil

PREPARATION:

1. Combine the spring mix and veggies in a large bowl.

2. In a small bowl, whisk together the vinegar, mustard, and salt. Stream in the oils and whisk continuously to emulsify. Toss salad with dressing and garnish with shaved Parmesan.

Serves 4-6

Adapted from L'Academie de Cuisine: Teen Cooking Camp 2017

Honey-Glazed Baby Carrots

INGREDIENTS:

2 tablespoons unsalted butter
1 (16-ounce) bag baby carrots
2 tablespoons honey
2 tablespoons brown sugar, packed
2 teaspoons fresh dill
2 teaspoons fresh thyme leaves

PREPARATION:

1. Melt butter in a large skillet over medium heat. Add carrots, honey, brown sugar, dill, and thyme and gently toss to combine, Cook, stirring occasionally, until carrots are tender, about 15 minutes.

2. Serve immediately.

Serves 4

Adapted from Damn Delicious website

POTATOES

Yukon Gold (Yellow)

Smooth-skinned and a bit waxy, this yellow potato has a light, buttery color on the inside. When cooked, it becomes flaky and a bit starchy. Use these when you're looking to mash or shred, but they're waxy enough to hold their shape if cooked in a soup or stew.

Sweet Potatoes (Yams)

Considerably sweeter than other potatoes, these are larger, heavier, starchier, and its coarse skin should be removed before eating. Sometimes sold as *yams*, these look and taste nothing like true yams. While roasting is a great way to bring out the sweetness, steaming will render them ever so moist and tender while retaining their signature flavor.

Baby Potatoes (New Potatoes or Creamers)

Immature potatoes—no matter if they're red, yellow or purple—are deemed *baby, new,* or *creamers*. These small potatoes are best cooked whole—boiled, steamed, roasted; keep the skins to add a colorful element to dishes.

Brown Russets (Idaho)

Russets are very starchy long and wide potatoes with skins that are dark, earthy, and rough; the skins should be removed before eating. Raw, they are firm, but when cooked, yield a light, fluffy interior. They are not great at retaining their shape so they are better for frying, baking, and mashing.

Red Potatoes (Red Bliss)

Red potatoes have a smooth, thin skin that makes a striking visual contrast against its white flesh. Its skin is edible; it's not necessary to peel or remove it after cooking. Like many waxy varieties, red potatoes are low in starch and won't produce a light, fluffy texture. However, they are prime candidates for boiling and roasting and work well in dishes that would benefit from a potato that holds its shape—even when sliced and diced—such as in salads and gratins.

Fingerlings

As their name suggests, fingerlings somewhat resemble fingers. Knobby, slim, firm, and short, these heirloom varieties are mainly found at farmers' markets or specialty gourmet shops. Fingerlings have distinctive flavors, usually nutty or earthy. They are uniquely shaped and are best cooked in a way that retains their shape—roasted, steamed, in salads, etc.

Potato Pancakes

INGREDIENTS:

2 pounds russet potatoes
1 medium onion
½ cup chopped scallions, including the light green part
1 large egg, beaten
Salt & pepper to taste
1 teaspoon vegetable oil

PREPARATION:

1. Peel the potatoes and place in cold water.

2. Coarsely grate the potatoes and onion with grater or a food processor. Place them in a fine-mesh strainer or tea towel and squeeze out all the water over a bowl. Carefully pour out the water, reserving the potato starch that settles to the bottom.

3. Mix the potato and onion with the potato starch. Add the scallions, egg, salt, and pepper.

4. Heat a griddle or nonstick pan and lightly coat with vegetable oil. Measure out about 2 tablespoons of the potato mixture and put it on the griddle, flatten with a large spatula, and fry for a few minutes until golden.

5. Flip the pancake over and brown the other side. Place on paper towels to cool. Serve immediately.

Serves 4

Adapted from L'Academie de Cuisine: Teen Cooking Camp 2017

Pommes Anna

INGREDIENTS:

2 pounds of small (slightly larger than a golf ball) Yukon Gold potatoes
½ cup (1 stick) unsalted butter
Salt & pepper
1 tablespoon dried thyme

PREPARATION:

1. Preheat oven to 350°F (177°C).

2. Slice potatoes crosswise into very thin rounds (less than ⅛ inch thick), placing them in a large bowl as you work.

3. Heat a sauté pan over medium-high heat. When the pan is hot, add a few pats of butter to coat the bottom of the pan. Once the butter is hot and starts to bubble, start to layer the potatoes in concentric circles starting from the center. In between each layer, season the potatoes well with salt, pepper, and thyme. The potatoes should stack about three layers high.

4. Cook the potatoes and press well with a spatula. The starch in the potatoes will act as a glue to keep them together. Once the potatoes start to brown on the bottom, place the pan in the oven for about 20 minutes.

5. Checking periodically while baking in the oven, continue to press the potato layers together. When the bottom of the potatoes are golden, carefully flip them over and finish cooking. When finished, gently slide the pancake out of the pan and slice wedges. Serve.

Serves 8

Adapted from L'Academie de Cuisine: Teen Cooking Camp 2017

Mashed Yukon Gold Potatoes

INGREDIENTS:

6-7 small Yukon Gold potatoes
¼ cup milk
¼ cup cream
2 tablespoons butter
¼ cup sour cream

PREPARATION:

1. Peel and cut potatoes into uniform slices about ¼ inch thick, and place in a pot of cold, salted water. Bring potatoes to a boil and cook for 8 minutes.

2. Strain and place potatoes (still in the strainer) over a bowl and allow to dry for about 8 minutes.

3. Meanwhile, combine milk and cream in a small saucepan, then bring to boil. Simmer for 3 minutes.

4. Place potatoes in a large bowl and pour in the milk and cream mixture. Add butter and sour cream.

5. Whip the potatoes with a hand mixer for about 7 minutes or until creamy. Serve.

Serves 4

Adapted from L'Academie de Cuisine: Teen Cooking Camp 2017

Seasoned Baked Potato Wedges

INGREDIENTS:

6 red potatoes, cut into wedges
2 tablespoons olive oil
2 teaspoons onion powder
2 teaspoons chili powder
1 teaspoon garlic powder
1 teaspoon garlic salt
Salt and pepper

PREPARATION:

1. Preheat oven to 375°F (190°C).

2. Spread potato wedges in a single layer on a baking sheet and drizzle with olive oil. In a small bowl, combine onion powder, chili powder, garlic powder, and garlic salt; sprinkle over potatoes and toss to coat evenly.

3. Bake until potatoes are tender, 30 to 35 minutes. Season with salt and pepper.

Serves 8

Adapted from the All Recipes website

Scalloped Potatoes

Scalloped Potatoes

INGREDIENTS:

Spray cooking oil
3 pounds of Yukon Gold potatoes, thinly sliced
½ onion, thinly sliced
9 tablespoons all-purpose flour, divided
6 tablespoons butter, diced and divided
Salt and ground black pepper to taste
3 cups whole milk

PREPARATION:

1. Preheat oven to 375°F (190°C). Spray a 9 x 13-inch baking dish with oil.

2. Spread ⅓ of the potato slices into the bottom of the prepared baking dish. Top with ⅓ of the onion slices. Sprinkle 3 tablespoons of flour over the potatoes and onions. Arrange 2 tablespoons of diced butter atop the flour. Season the entire layer with salt and pepper. Repeat layering twice more.

3. Heat milk in a saucepan until warm. Pour enough warm milk over the mixture in the baking dish until the top of the liquid is level with the final layer of potatoes.

4. Bake in preheated oven until potatoes are tender, 45 to 60 minutes.

Serves 6

Adapted from the All Recipes website

Stresa Italy

ENTREES

Chicken and Rice Skillet

INGREDIENTS:

Cooking spray
1 medium onion, chopped
2 teaspoons olive oil
1 cup uncooked long grain rice
2 garlic cloves, minced
1 (14.5-ounce) can reduced-sodium chicken broth
1 (14-ounce) can diced tomatoes and green chilies, undrained (Rotel brand tomatoes and green chilies work well)
3 tablespoons water
½ teaspoon ground cumin
½ teaspoon dried oregano
2 cups cooked chicken breasts cut into 1-inch cubes
1 cup frozen peas

PREPARATION:

1. In a large nonstick skillet coated with cooking spray, sauté onion in oil until tender.

2. Add rice and garlic; cook and stir for 3-4 minutes or until rice is lightly browned. Add the broth, tomatoes, water, cumin, and oregano. Bring to a boil. Reduce heat; cover and simmer for 15 to 20 minutes or until rice is tender. Add chicken and peas; heat through, about 5 minutes.

Serves 4

Adapted from the Taste of Home website

Creamy Garlic Mushroom Chicken

INGREDIENTS:

¼ cup plus 2 teaspoons all-purpose flour, divided
1 pound (4 pieces) thin-sliced boneless chicken breast
½ teaspoon salt, divided
¼ teaspoon ground pepper
2 tablespoons extra-virgin olive oil, divided
8 ounces button mushrooms, quartered
2 cloves of garlic minced
1/2 cup chicken stock
½ cup half-and-half
¼ cup shredded Parmesan cheese
2 tablespoons chopped fresh parsley

PREPARATION:

1. Place ¼ cup flour in a shallow dish.

2. Sprinkle chicken with ¼ teaspoon salt and pepper. Coat chicken in flour, shaking off the excess. Discard any leftover flour. Wash hands thoroughly.

3. Heat 1 tablespoon oil in a large skillet over medium-high heat. Add the chicken and cook, turning once, until golden brown and cooked through, 5 to 8 minutes per side. Transfer the chicken to a plate; cover to keep warm.

4. Add the remaining 1 tablespoon oil to the pan. Reduce heat to medium and add mushrooms and the remaining ¼ teaspoon salt. Stir frequently until the mushrooms begin to brown and soften, 4 to 6 minutes. Stir in garlic and cook until fragrant, about 30 seconds more. Sprinkle the remaining 2 teaspoons of flour over the mushroom mixture and stir to coat. Add chicken stock and cook until sauce has thickened.

5. Add half-and-half, stirring until the sauce is bubbling and thickened, 1 to 2 minutes. Return chicken to pan and heat for about 5 minutes. Remove from heat and serve topped with Parmesan and parsley.

Serves 2

Adapted from the eatingwell website

Thai Chicken Stir Fry

Thai Chicken Stir-Fry

INGREDIENTS:

2 tablespoons peanut or canola oil, divided
1pound boneless, skinless chicken breast, trimmed, cut into 1-inch pieces
3 scallions, cut into 1-inch pieces
2 small fresh red chiles, thinly sliced (optional)
2 cloves garlic, thinly sliced
1 large zucchini, quartered lengthwise and sliced into ½-inch pieces
2 tablespoons fish sauce
2 teaspoons lime juice
2 teaspoons molasses
2 teaspoons cornstarch
½ cup toasted cashews
¼ cup chopped fresh basil, preferably Thai

PREPARATION:

1. Heat 1 tablespoon oil in a large, flat-bottom, carbon-steel wok or large skillet over medium-high heat. Add chicken and cook, stirring occasionally, until just cooked through, 4 to 5 minutes. Transfer to a plate.

2. Add the remaining 1 tablespoon oil, scallions, and chiles (if using); cook and stir until the scallions start to soften, about 30 seconds. Add garlic and zucchini and cook, stirring until the zucchini is just tender, about 3 minutes.

3. Meanwhile, whisk fish sauce, lime juice, molasses, and cornstarch in a small bowl. Add the sauce and the chicken (along with accumulated juice) into the pan; cook, stirring frequently until the sauce is bubbling and thickened. Remove from the heat and stir in cashews and basil. Serve.

Serves 4

Adapted from Eating Well Test Kitchen. eatingwell.com

Chicken Marengo

INGREDIENTS:

Salt and pepper
4 chicken breasts, bone-in
¼ cup all-purpose flour
¼ cup extra-virgin olive oil
1 small shallot diced
2 cloves of garlic, minced
6 ounces button mushrooms, sliced and stems removed
1½ cup beef stock
1 (14.5-ounce) can petite diced tomatoes
½ teaspoon dry thyme

PREPARATION:

1. Preheat oven to 350°F (177°C).

2. Salt and pepper chicken breasts then dredge in flour until coated. Shake off excess flour.

3. Heat oil in sauté pan until hot but not smoking. Sauté chicken breasts on each side for about 2 minutes. Place the chicken in an oven-proof pan and bake 15 minutes.

4. Meanwhile, sauté shallots until they soften. Add garlic and sauté for another 30 seconds. Add mushrooms and cook until moisture is no longer leaked. Add beef stock and boil until liquid is reduced by half, about 1 minute. Add tomatoes and thyme and simmer for 5 minutes.

5. Remove chicken breasts from oven and add them to the sauce. Simmer chicken with sauce for about 5 minutes, then serve. (Brown Rice goes well with this dish.)

Serves 4

Adapted from My Mom's a Good Cooker website

Blackened Chicken

INGREDIENTS:

½ teaspoon paprika
⅛ teaspoon salt
¼ teaspoon cayenne pepper
¼ teaspoon ground cumin
¼ teaspoon dried thyme
⅛ teaspoon ground white pepper
⅛ teaspoon onion powder
Spray oil
2 skinless, boneless chicken breast halves

PREPARATION:

1. Preheat to 350°F (175°C). Lightly grease a baking sheet.

2. Mix together the paprika, salt, cayenne, cumin, thyme, white pepper, and onion powder. Oil the chicken breasts with cooking spray on both sides, then coat the chicken breasts evenly with the spice mixture.

3. Heat a cast iron skillet until very hot. Place the chicken in the hot pan and cook for 1 minute. Turn and cook 1 minute on the other side. Place the breasts on the prepared baking sheet.

4. Bake in preheated oven until no longer pink in the center and the juices run clear, about 10 minutes. Remove and serve.

Serves 2

Adapted from www.allrecipes.com

Easy Kung Pao Chicken

INGREDIENTS:

1½ pounds chicken tenders cut into 1-inch pieces
1½ tablespoons cornstarch
3 teaspoons vegetable oil
3 tablespoons chopped green onions (include the light green part)
3 cloves garlic, minced
1 teaspoon crushed red pepper flakes (more/less to suit your taste)
1½ teaspoons powdered ginger
3 tablespoons white wine vinegar
3 tablespoons reduced salt soy sauce
⅓ cup sriracha hot chili sauce
½ cup honey roasted peanuts

PREPARATION:

1. Combine chicken and cornstarch in a bowl and toss until chicken is coated.

2. Heat oil in large nonstick sauté pan (no wok needed). Add chicken and stir-fry for about 5 minutes over medium heat until chicken is cooked through. Remove chicken to a small bowl and set aside.

3. Return sauté pan to heat and add green onions, garlic, red pepper and ginger. Sauté for 15 to 20 seconds. Add this to the bowl with chicken.

4. Combine vinegar and soy sauce in a small bowl and stir well. Add to sauté pan with along with the chicken mixture and stir well. Add sriracha sauce and combine thoroughly. Add in peanuts. Heat thoroughly. Serve with brown rice.

Serves 4

Adapted from My Mom's a Good Cooker website

Sheet-Pan Chicken Fajitas

INGREDIENTS:

1 pound boneless, skinless chicken breasts
2 tablespoons extra-virgin olive oil
1 tablespoon chili powder
2 teaspoons ground cumin
1 teaspoon garlic powder
¾ teaspoon salt
1 large red bell pepper, sliced
1 large yellow bell pepper, sliced
2 cups sliced onion (about 1 large)
1 tablespoon lime juice
8 corn tortillas, warmed
1 lime cut into wedges

PREPARATION:

1. Preheat oven to 400°F (204°C). Coat a large rimmed baking sheet with cooking spray.

2. Cut chicken breasts in half horizontally, then slice crosswise into strips. Combine oil, chili powder, cumin, garlic powder, and salt in a large bowl. Add the chicken and stir to coat with the spice mixture. Add bell peppers and onions and stir to combine. Transfer the chicken and vegetables to the prepared baking sheet and spread in an even layer.

3. Roast on the middle rack for 15 minutes. Leave the pan there and turn the broiler to high. Broil until the chicken is cooked through and the vegetables are browning in spots, about 5 minutes more. Remove from oven. Drizzle the lime juice over the pan.

4. Serve the chicken and vegetables in warmed tortillas accompanied by lime wedges and topped with cilantro, sour cream, avocado, and/or pico de gallo, if desired.

Serves 4

Adapted from the eatingwell website

Stir-Fried Chicken & Vegetables

INGREDIENTS:

3 tablespoons cooking oil, divided (vegetable, canola, or peanut)
1 boneless chicken breast and 2 boneless thighs
1 medium onion, sliced
1 carrot, cut thinly on a diagonal
1 red pepper, sliced
1 cup button mushrooms, sliced or quartered
1 small zucchini, peeled and sliced
1 clove garlic, sliced thin
1 teaspoon powdered ginger
3 tablespoons soy sauce
1 tablespoon sesame oil

MARINADE:

3 tablespoons chili sauce
2 tablespoons honey

PREPARATION:

1. Combine chili sauce and honey to prepare the marinade. Pour over chicken and marinate for 20 minutes

2. Heat large sauté pan over high heat. Add 2 tablespoons of oil to the pan and heat. Add enough marinated chicken to cover the bottom of the pan without crowding. Brown the chicken on all sides until cooked through. Remove chicken and set aside. Cook the rest of the chicken in batches until all of it is cooked. Set aside.

3. Add the remaining oil to pan and cook the vegetables: first cook the onions until brown, then carrots, peppers, mushrooms, zucchini, garlic, and ginger. Stir-fry for 3 minutes.

4. Add cooked chicken, stir for 2 minutes. Serve over Jasmine Rice (next page).

Serves 4

Steamed Jasmine Rice

INGREDIENTS:

1 cup jasmine rice
1 cup water
Pinch salt to season

PREPARATION:

1. Rinse rice with water twice. Drain completely.

2. Place rice, water, and salt in a small pot and bring to a boil.

3. Cover and reduce heat to medium-low and steam for 25 or 30 minutes until water is completely absorbed.

4. Remove from heat. Fluff with fork. Top with the stir-fried chicken and vegetables

Serves 4

Stir Fry chicken and vegetables and the Jasmine Rice are adapted from L'Academie de Cuisine: Teen Cooking Camp 2017

Easy-to-Stuff Manicotti

INGREDIENTS:

1 (8-ounce) package manicotti shells
1 pound ground beef
½ cup chopped onions
1 (24-ounce) jar marinara sauce
14 pieces string cheese
1½ cups shredded part-skim mozzarella cheese

PREPARATION:

1. Cook manicotti according to package directions. Meanwhile, in a large skillet, cook beef and onion over medium heat until meat is no longer pink. Drain the beef then stir in marinara sauce. Spread half of the meat sauce into a greased 9 x 13-inch baking dish.

2. Drain manicotti and stuff each shell with a piece of string cheese. Place over meat sauce; top with remaining sauce. Cover and bake at 350°F (177°C) for 25 to 30 minutes or until heated through.

3. Sprinkle with mozzarella cheese. Bake 5 to 10 minutes longer or until cheese is melted.

Serves 6

Adapted from RDA Enthusiast Brands, LLC

Fettuccine Primavera

INGREDIENTS:

4 ounces uncooked fettuccine
1 tablespoon canola oil
½ cup fresh cauliflower
½ cup fresh snow peas
½ cup fresh broccoli florets
¼ cup julienned carrots
½ cup julienned zucchini
¼ cup julienned sweet red pepper
2 to 3 garlic cloves, minced
⅓ cup chicken broth
¼ cup grated Romano cheese

PREPARATION:

1. Cook fettuccine according to package directions. Meanwhile, pour oil into a skillet or wok and stir-fry the cauliflower, peas, broccoli, and carrots for 2 minutes.

2. Add the zucchini, red pepper, and garlic; stir-fry until vegetables are tender-crisp (heated through but still have a snap to them). Stir in broth. Reduce heat; cover and simmer for 2 minutes.

3. Drain fettuccine; add to vegetable mixture and toss to coat. Sprinkle with cheese.

Serves 2

Adapted from RDA Enthusiast Brands, LLC

Cheesy Quesadillas

INGREDIENTS:

4 (8-inch) flour tortillas, warmed
1½ cups shredded Mexican cheese blend
½ cup salsa

PREPARATION:

1. Place the tortillas on a greased baking sheet. Combine the cheese and salsa; spread on half of each tortilla. Fold over.

2. Broil 4 inches from the heat for 3 minutes on each side or until golden brown. Cut into wedges and serve.

Serves 2

Adapted from Taste of Home website

Quaker Oatmeal Prize-Winning Meatloaf

INGREDIENTS:

Spray oil
1½ pounds lean ground beef (or turkey)
¾ cup Quaker® Oats
¾ cup finely chopped onion
½ cup tomato sauce
1 egg, lightly beaten
1 tablespoon Worcestershire sauce
½ teaspoon garlic powder
½ teaspoon salt
¼ teaspoon black pepper

PREPARATION:

1. Heat oven to 350°F (177°C). Spray loaf pan with oil.

2. Combine all ingredients in large bowl; mix lightly but thoroughly. Add to loaf pan.

3. Bake 50 to 55 minutes or until meatloaf is done (160°F/71°C for beef, 170°F/77°C for turkey). Remove meatloaf from pan and let rest for 10 minutes before slicing.

Serves 6

Adapted from the Epicurious website

Homemade Pizza

PIZZA DOUGH INGREDIENTS:

3½ to 4 cups bread flour
1 teaspoon sugar
1 envelope instant dry yeast
2 teaspoons salt
1½ cups hot water (110°F/43°C).
2 tablespoons plus 2 teaspoons olive oil

PREPARATION:

1. Combine the bread flour, sugar, yeast, and salt in the bowl of a stand mixer and combine.

2. While the mixer is running, add the water and 2 tablespoons of the oil and beat until the dough forms into a ball. If the dough is sticky, add additional flour, 1 tablespoon at a time, until the dough comes together in a solid ball. If the dough is too dry, add additional water, 1 tablespoon at a time.

3. Scrape the bowl and place the dough onto a lightly floured surface. Gently knead into a smooth, firm ball.

4. Grease a large bowl with the remaining 2 teaspoons olive oil, add the dough, cover the bowl with plastic wrap and put it in a warm area to let it double in size, about 1 hour.

5. Turn the dough out onto a lightly floured surface and divide it into 2 equal pieces. Cover each with a clean kitchen towel or plastic wrap and let them rest for 10 minutes.

Nothing like homemade. YUMMY !

TOMATO SAUCE INGREDIENTS:

1 tablespoon olive oil
1 medium-sized onion, diced
2 cloves garlic, minced
1 (28-ounce) can whole tomatoes, drained and chopped
1 (8-ounce) can tomato sauce
1 (6-ounce) can tomato paste
½ teaspoon oregano
½ teaspoon basil
½ teaspoon thyme
½ teaspoon fennel seeds
2 bay leaves
Salt and pepper to taste

PREPARATION:

1. Heat the olive oil over medium-low heat in a heavy saucepan. Add the onion, cooking until soft but not browned. Add the garlic. Cook 1 minute. Add drained tomatoes, tomato sauce, tomato paste, and all of the spices.

2. Bring this mixture to a boil, and then reduce heat to a simmer. Simmer 45 to 60 minutes. This makes the sauce naturally sweet.

ASSEMBLING THE PIZZA:

Roll out the dough to make two 14-inch pizza crusts. Pour and spread ½ cup of the sauce onto each crust. Top the pizzas with shredded mozzarella cheese (more or less cheese depending on taste, 2 cups is a middle ground), preferred toppings, and bake for 15 to 20 minutes.

Serves 6

Adapted from Food Network (dough) and Joel Olson(Sauce)L'Academie de Cuisine

Oven-Fried Chicken

INGREDIENTS:

Vegetable cooking spray
2 cups low fat sour cream
4 cloves garlic, minced
4 cups crushed cornflakes cereal
4 tablespoons crushed dried rosemary
3 tablespoons dried sage
3 tablespoons garlic powder
Salt and pepper to taste
6 chicken drumsticks(with skin)
6 bone-in chicken breast halves (with skin)

PREPARATION:

1. Preheat the oven to 350°F (175 °C). Place a cooling rack on top of a large cookie sheet. Spray the rack with vegetable cooking spray.

2. In a medium bowl, mix together sour cream and minced garlic. In another bowl, stir together the cornflake crumbs, rosemary, sage, garlic powder, salt, and pepper. Coat the chicken with the sour cream mixture, then roll in the cornflake mixture. Arrange chicken pieces on top of the cooling rack.

3. Bake for 60 minutes in the preheated oven until meat is no longer pink and juices run clear.

Serves 6

Adapted from All Recipes website

Baked Chicken Nuggets

INGREDIENTS:

Spray cooking oil
3 skinless, boneless chicken breasts
1 cup Italian seasoned bread crumbs
½ cup grated Parmesan cheese
1 teaspoon salt
1 teaspoon dried thyme
1 tablespoon dried basil
½ cup butter, melted

PREPARATION:

1. Preheat oven to 400°F (204 °C) and lightly spray a cookie sheet with oil.

2. Cut chicken breasts into 1½ inch pieces. In a medium bowl, mix together bread crumbs, cheese, salt, thyme, and basil. Mix well. Put melted butter in a bowl or dish for dipping.

3. Dip chicken pieces into the melted butter first, then coat with the breadcrumb mixture. Place the well-coated chicken pieces on the cookie sheet in a single layer, and bake in preheated oven for 20 minutes.

Serves 6

Adapted from All Recipes website

Buffalo Wings

Buffalo Wings

INGREDIENTS:

Spray cooking oil
¾ cup all-purpose flour
¼ teaspoon cayenne pepper
½ teaspoon garlic powder
½ teaspoon salt
20 chicken wings
½ cup melted butter
½ cup hot pepper sauce

PREPARATION:

1. Line a baking sheet with aluminum foil and lightly grease with cooking spray. Place the flour, cayenne pepper, garlic powder, and salt into a large resealable plastic bag or container with a tight-fitting lid and shake to mix. Add the chicken wings, seal, and toss until well-coated with the flour mixture. Place the wings onto the prepared baking sheet and place into the refrigerator. Refrigerate at least 45 minutes.

2. Preheat oven to 400°F (204°C).

3. Whisk together the melted butter and hot sauce in a small bowl. Dip the wings into the butter mixture and place back on the baking sheet. Bake in preheated oven for 45 minutes, turn the wings over halfway through, until the chicken is no longer pink in the center and is crispy on the outside.

Serves 4

Adapted from All Recipes website

Lasagna Cupcakes

INGREDIENTS:

Spray oil
⅓ pound ground beef
Salt and ground black pepper, to taste
36 wonton wrappers (found in the freezer section of grocery store)
1¾ cups grated Parmesan cheese, divided
1¾ cups shredded mozzarella cheese, divided
¾ cup ricotta cheese, divided
1 cup marinara sauce (purchased or made from scratch)
¼ cup chopped fresh basil

PREPARATION:

1. Preheat oven to 375°F (190°C). Prepare muffin cups with cooking spray.

2. Cook ground beef in hot skillet until browned and crumbly, 5 to 7 minutes. Season with salt and pepper. Drain and discard grease from the beef.

3. Cut wonton wrappers into 2¼-inch circles with a biscuit cutter or rim of a similar-sized drinking glass. Press one wonton into the bottom of each muffin cup. Add 1 teaspoon each of Parmesan, mozzarella, and ricotta cheese to each muffin cup; top with 1 teaspoon each of ground beef and marinara. Divide remaining ground beef, marinara, ricotta, and 1 cup of Parmesan and 1 cup of mozzarella in half. Add second wonton wrapper to each muffin cup. Divide the first portion of the divided ingredients evenly over second wonton in each muffin cup. Repeat process with remaining half of divided portion.

4. Top each muffin with remaining Parmesan and mozzarella

5. Bake in preheated oven until edges of lasagna cupcakes are browned; 18 to 20 minutes. Remove from oven and let them rest for 5 minutes before running a knife around the edges of each muffin cup to loosen and remove. Garnish with fresh basil and serve.

Makes 12 cupcakes

Adapted from All Recipes website

Chicken Pita Sandwiches

INGREDIENTS:

1 (8-ounce) package cream cheese, softened
3 tablespoons whole milk
1 tablespoon lemon juice
2 cups cooked chicken, cubed
½ cup green pepper, chopped
2 tablespoons green onions, chopped
1 teaspoon ground mustard
½ teaspoon dried thyme
½ teaspoon salt
⅛ teaspoon pepper
¼ cup chopped walnuts
6 pita pocket halves

PREPARATION:

1. In a large bowl, beat the cream cheese, milk, and lemon juice until smooth. Stir in the chicken, green pepper, onions, mustard, thyme, salt, and pepper; refrigerate until chilled, about 15minutes.

2. Just before serving, stir in walnuts. Spoon about ½ cup filling into each pita half and serve.

Serves 3

Adapted from RDA Enthusiast Brand LLC

Quick Chili Mac

INGREDIENTS:

1 (12-ounce) package uncooked elbow macaroni
1 pound ground beef
1 small green pepper, chopped
1 small onion, chopped
1 (14.5-ounce) can petite diced tomatoes
1 tablespoon chili powder
2 teaspoons cumin
2 (15-ounce) cans chili beans
1 (15-ounce) can corn
Salt and pepper to taste
1 cup shredded cheddar cheese

PREPARATION:

1. Cook and drain macaroni according to package directions.

2. Meanwhile, in a large skillet, cook beef, pepper, and onion over medium heat until beef is no longer pink.

3. Add tomatoes, chili powder, and cumin to the beef mixture simmer for about 10 minutes

4. Stir in chili beans, corn, and macaroni; heat thoroughly.

5. Sprinkle with cheese and allow cheese to melt before serving.

Serves 6

Adapted from RDA Enthusiast Brand, LLC

Pigs in a Blanket

INGREDIENTS:

1 (8-ounce) tube refrigerated crescent rolls
4 beef hot dogs, cut into thirds
1 egg, lightly beaten
1 tablespoon water

PREPARATION:

1. Preheat oven to 375°F (190°C).

2. Separate crescent dough into triangles. Place hot dog pieces at wide ends of triangles and roll up. Place on an ungreased baking sheet. Combine egg and water; brush over rolls.

3. Bake 12-15 minutes or until golden brown.

Serves 4

Adapted from RDA Enthusiast Brand, LLC

Cheddar Mac & Cheese

INGREDIENTS:

1 (16-ounce) package elbow macaroni
½ cup butter, cubed
½ cup all-purpose flour
½ teaspoon onion powder
½ teaspoon ground chipotle pepper
¼ teaspoon pepper
¼ teaspoon salt
4 cups 2% milk
1 cup shredded cheddar cheese

PREPARATION:

1. Cook and drain macaroni according to package directions.

2. Meanwhile, in a large saucepan, melt butter over medium heat. Stir in flour, onion powder, chipotle pepper, pepper, and salt until ingredients are combined.

3. Gradually whisk in milk. Bring to a boil, stirring constantly until thickened, 6 to 8 minutes.

4. Remove from heat; stir in cheese until melted. Add to pasta and stir until mixture is smooth. Serve.

Serves 8

Adapted from RDA Enthusiast Brand, LLC

Tacos

INGREDIENTS:

2 pounds ground beef
2 tablespoons chopped onion
1 (14.5-ounce) can/box beef broth
1 (8-ounce) can tomato sauce
¼ cup chili powder
2 tablespoons paprika
1 tablespoon ground cumin
1 teaspoon garlic powder
¼ teaspoon cayenne pepper (or to taste)
½ teaspoon pepper
½ teaspoon lime juice
¼ teaspoon onion powder
¼ teaspoon sugar
¼ teaspoon salt
Taco shells or flour tortillas
Shredded cheese and salsa

PREPARATION:

1. In a large skillet, cook the beef and onion over medium heat until meat is no longer pink, then drain meat and return to the pan. Stir in all the other ingredients except for the taco shells/tortillas, cheese, and salsa. Bring to a boil. Reduce heat, then cover and simmer for 10 minutes.

2. Serve in taco shells or tortillas with shredded cheese and salsa.

Serves 8

Adapted from RDA Enthusiast Brand, LLC

DESSERTS

———

Tropical Carrot Cake

CAKE INGREDIENTS:

3 large eggs
¾ cup canola oil
¾ cup buttermilk
2 cups all-purpose flour
2 cups sugar
2 teaspoons baking soda
2 teaspoons ground cinnamon
½ teaspoon salt
2 teaspoons vanilla extract
2 cups carrots, finely shredded
1 cup raisins
1 (8-ounce) can crushed pineapple, undrained
1 cup chopped walnuts
1 cup sweetened shredded coconut

FROSTING INGREDIENTS:

1 (8-ounce) package cream cheese, softened
4+ cups confectioners' (powdered) sugar
1 to 2 tablespoons heavy whipping cream
1 teaspoon vanilla extract

PREPARATION:

In a large bowl, beat eggs, oil, and buttermilk. In another bowl, combine flour, sugar, baking soda, cinnamon, and salt; add to egg mixture and stir well. Stir in vanilla, carrots, raisins, pineapple, walnuts, and coconut; mix well. Pour into a greased 9x13 inch baking pan. Bake at 350°F (177°C) for 45 to 50 minutes.

For frosting, beat all ingredients in a bowl until smooth. Add more sugar if too runny, more cream if too stiff.

Makes 12 servings

Adapted from Taste of Home website

Frozen Berry & Yogurt Pops

INGREDIENTS:

10 (3-ounce) plastic or paper cups
2¾ cups fat-free honey Greek yogurt
1 cup mixed fresh berries
¼ cup water
2 tablespoons sugar
10 wooden pop sticks

PREPARATION:

1. Fill each cup with about ¼ cup yogurt. Place berries, water, and sugar in a food processor and pulse until berries are finely chopped. Spoon 1½ tablespoons berry mixture into each cup. Stir gently with a pop stick to swirl.

2. Top cups with foil; insert pop sticks through foil. Freeze until firm.

Makes 10 pops

Adapted from RDA Enthusiast Brands, LLC

Dark Chocolate Mousse

INGREDIENTS:

5¼ ounces bittersweet chocolate, coarsely chopped
14 ounces cold heavy cream
3 large egg whites
2 tablespoons of sugar
Sweetened whipped cream, for garnish
Shaved bittersweet chocolate, for garnish

PREPARATION:

1. Place chocolate in a large bowl. Set the bowl over a pan of simmering water. Stir chocolate until melted. Turn off the heat and let stand.

2. Add cream to a deep bowl and beat until it forms soft peaks. Set aside at room temperature. With a mixer, whip egg whites until soft peaks have formed. Gradually add the sugar and continue whipping until firm.

3. Remove the chocolate from the bowl and, using a whisk, fold in the egg whites all at once. When the whites are almost completely incorporated, fold in the whipped cream. Cover the mousse with plastic wrap and refrigerate for 60 minutes or until set. Serve in goblets topped with more whipped cream and shaved chocolate, if desired.

Serves 6

Adapted from Bobby Flay on Food Network

Peach Puffs

INGREDIENTS:

1 sheet frozen puff pastry, thawed
2 cups peaches, peeled and thinly sliced, or unsweetened frozen peaches, thawed
1 tablespoon sugar
3 ounces cream cheese, softened
2 tablespoons confectioners' (powdered) sugar
½ teaspoon vanilla extract
2 cups whipped topping
6 fresh raspberries

PREPARATION:

1. On a lightly floured surface; roll pastry to ⅛ inch thickness. Cut out circles with a floured 3½-inch round cookie cutter. Place circles on an ungreased baking sheet. You should have 12 circles. Bake at 400°F (204°C) for 8 to 10 minutes or until golden brown. Remove to wire rack and cool.

2. In a large bowl, toss peaches with sugar; set aside. In a small bowl, beat cream cheese, confectioners' sugar, and vanilla until smooth. Fold in the whipped topping.

3. Peel pastry circles apart to get two halves. Spread about 2 tablespoons of cream cheese mixture over the bottom half of each; replace tops. Spread about 1 tablespoon of cream cheese mixture on the top of each. Arrange peach slices in an overlapping circular pattern on the cream cheese layer. Garnish each with a raspberry.

Serves 6

Adapted from RDA Enthusiast Brands, LLC

Basic Cupcakes

INGREDIENTS:

2½ cup all-purpose flour
1½ cup sugar
⅛ cup cocoa powder
1½ teaspoon baking soda
1 teaspoon salt
1 cup vegetable or canola oil
1 cup buttermilk
2 large eggs
2 teaspoons white vinegar
1 teaspoon vanilla extract

PREPARATION:

1. Preheat the oven to 350°F (177°C).

2. Place all dry ingredient—flour, sugar, cocoa powder, baking soda, and salt—in the bowl of a stand mixer and mix with a paddle attachment at the lowest speed for 1 or 2 minutes.

3. Combine canola oil, buttermilk, eggs, vinegar, and vanilla in a medium bowl or large pourable measuring cup.

4. With mixer on low speed, gradually add wet ingredients to dry. Increase speed to medium and mix until batter is smooth.

5. Pour or scoop batter into lined cupcake pans until ⅔ full and bake 18 to 20 minutes or until toothpick inserted in the center comes out clean. Frosting options are on the next page.

Makes 12 cupcakes

Adapted from L'Academie de Cuisine: Teen Cooking Camp 2017

Vanilla Buttercream Frosting

INGREDIENTS:

8 ounces unsalted butter, room temperature
2 pounds of confectioners' (powdered) sugar
½ cup heavy cream
1 teaspoon vanilla extract

PREPARATION:

Place butter in bowl. Beat at medium speed. Reduce speed to low and alternate adding sugar and cream. Add vanilla. Scrape bowl and increase speed to high. Beat for at least 2 minutes until light and fluffy. Frost cupcakes.

Cream Cheese Frosting

INGREDIENTS:

12 ounces cream cheese, room temperature
12 ounces unsalted butter, room temperature
1½ teaspoon vanilla extract
16 ounces confectioners' (powdered) sugar

PREPARATION:

Beat cream cheese and butter at medium speed in mixer until completely combined with no lumps. Add vanilla and mix until combined. Slowly add sugar at low speed, then increase speed to medium and beat until light and fluffy. Frost cupcakes.

Adapted from L'Academie de Cuisine: Teen Cooking Camp 2017

Key Lime Cookies

INGREDIENTS:

Parchment paper
1½ cups all-purpose flour
1 teaspoon baking powder
Salt
½ cup unsalted butter
1 cup sugar
1 egg
2 tablespoons key lime juice

PREPARATION:

1. Preheat oven to 350°F (177°C) and cover a cookie sheet with parchment paper.

2. Combine flour, baking powder, and salt, and set aside.

3. Beat cream and unsalted butter and sugar on medium speed until mixed together. Add egg and stir until just mixed. On low speed, add key lime juice and beat until creamed.

4. Add flour, baking powder, and salt mixture on slow setting until dough comes together.

5. Roll dough into small (about 1inch) balls and place on cookie sheet. Bake 12-15 minutes until set and edges are golden brown.

Makes 12 cookies

Adapted from www.finediningsolutions.com

Very Berry Crème Caramel

INGREDIENTS:

2 cups of cream
8 large egg yolks
½ cup sugar + 4 teaspoons
1 teaspoon vanilla extract
16 fresh berries (raspberry, blueberry, blackberry, etc.)
4 (4-ounce) ramekins
Roasting pan
8 teaspoon sugar, for finish

PREPARATION:

1. Preheat oven to 325°F (163°C). Place cream in medium saucepan bring to just short of simmering. Remove from heat.

2. In a large bowl, beat egg yolks and ½ sugar until well blended. Gradually stir in the cream; start with just a little bit in order to "temper" the egg mix. Add vanilla, return the mixture to the pan, and place over low heat stirring for about 2 minutes.

3. Strain through a strainer into a bowl and then pour into a container that has a pour spout or lip.

4. Place at least 4 berries into each ramekin. Also, place a cotton towel into the bottom of a roasting pan. Place ramekins onto towel and pour custard into each ramekin, until about ¾ full. Add very hot water to the roasting pan halfway up the side of each ramekin.

5. Bake 35 to 40 minutes or until custards are set but still shaky in the center. (Deeper ramekins will take longer).

6. Cool and refrigerate. Just before serving, coat each custard with one teaspoon sugar. Carefully use a culinary torch to melt the sugar. You can also broil for 30 to 40 seconds in oven. In a minute or so, the top will harden. You can place in the refrigerator for another 15 minutes to help harden the sugar on top; any longer than that and the sugar will start to get wet.

Serves 4

Adapted from L'Academie de Cuisine: Teen Cooking Camp 2017

Strawberry Shortcake

FILLING INGREDIENTS:

2 cups strawberries, hulled and chopped
¼ cup sugar
1 teaspoon lemon, lime, or orange juice

SHORTCAKE INGREDIENTS:

2 cups all-purpose flour
2 tablespoons sugar
2 teaspoons baking powder
½ teaspoon salt
2 tablespoons cold unsalted butter, cut into pieces
1½ teaspoons lemon, lime, or orange zest
¾ cup heavy whipping cream
¼ cup milk

PREPARATION:

1. Combine the strawberries, sugar and fruit juice of your choice to make the filling. Set aside. (Filling can be made the day before and refrigerated).

2. For the shortcakes, sift together the flour, sugar, baking powder, and salt. Using two forks or a pastry cutter, "cut in" the butter and fruit zest to the mix until it resembles coarse crumbs. Stir in cream to make soft dough.

3. On a floured surface, form the dough into a ball then pat it out to ½ inch thick. Cut out desired size rounds and place on a greased baking sheet. Gently form scraps into a balls and repeat.

4. Brush the top of the rounds with milk and bake at 400°F (204°C) for 15-20 minutes until puffed and golden. After cooling completely, slice each shortcake in two pieces horizontally. Fill with strawberries and cream and serve.

Serves 4

Adapted from L'Academie de Cuisine: Teen Cooking Camp 2017

Cooking Terms

Beat: To make smooth using a rapid lifting or circular motion.

Blanch: To immerse food items into boiling water for a short time (usually only 30 seconds) and then plunge into an ice water bath to stop further cooking. This technique is often used for vegetables to brighten or set the color and flavor before freezing. It is also used for crisp but tender vegetables for a dish, shortening the cooking time later, or to loosen skins (as for tomatoes or peaches). Fish and meat may also be blanched. This technique is sometimes referred to as **parboiling** or **scalding.**

Blend: Combining two or more ingredients until they are well mixed and smooth.

Boil: Heating a liquid until bubbles break on the surface—this would be 212°F (100°C) for water at sea level. This term also applies to cooking food in a boiling liquid.

Braise: A moist-heat cooking method for less-tender cuts of meat and poultry that begins with browning the food item(s) in fat, then simmering, tightly covered, in a small amount of flavorful liquid for a lengthy amount of time. This process helps develop the flavor and tenderizes the meat or poultry. The braising liquid is often then thickened to make a sauce or gravy. Braising can be done on stovetop or in the oven. This method is often used for pot roast or beef stew.

Broil: A dry-heat method used to cook food directly under or over a heat source. For example, food can be broiled in an electric or gas oven under direct heat, or on a barbeque grill over the direct heat of charcoal, gas, electric, or hardwood.

Cream: To make an ingredient or mixture smooth, soft, and "creamy" with an electric mixer or spoon. This term generally applies to creaming a fat such as butter with sugar to make a smooth, light mixture.

Dilute: To lessen the strength or concentration of by adding a liquid or water.

Dissolve: To incorporate dry ingredients (such as sugar, salt, yeast, or gelatin) into a liquid, generally by stirring to such a thorough extent that no evidence of the granular state of the ingredient remains.

Double Boiler: A cooking pot arrangement of two nested pans—with the top pan fitting part of the way inside of the bottom—with a lid on the top pan. A similar arrangement can be devised with a heat-proof bowl (glass or stainless steel) set on top of a smaller pan. In both examples, water is brought to a simmer over direct heat in the bottom pan which gently heats the mixture in the upper pan/bowl for slow, even cooking. This is also called a **bain marie.**

Fillet: A boneless piece of meat or fish.

Fold: Using a flexible scraper, whisk, or spoon, move the utensil down through the center of the mixture and gently move it up the side, turning the bowl a quarter turn after each complete stroke. Fold the mixture just until the mixture is blended—do not overmix—because this technique is designed to mix light ingredients with firmer ingredients.

Giblets: This term refers to the gizzard, heart, and liver (and sometimes includes the neck) of a chicken. The giblets are generally found in a package inside the body cavity of the chicken.

Grate: To create small particles or thin shreds by rubbing a whole or large item of food (for example, a block of cheese or a whole carrot) against the various coarse or notched cutting surfaces of a grater. A food processor fitted with a metal knife blade can do this with certain foods such as hard cheeses or dry bread crumbs; fitted with a shredding disk, a food processor can create long thin strips of various cheeses, carrots, etc. Grating or shredding cheese in the food processor is most successful when the cheese is refrigerated first for firmness. See also the term **shred**.

Grill: To cook food on a grill over the direct heat of charcoal, gas, electric, or hardwood. The food is generally not enclosed with a lid or cover. In some locales, the term **barbeque** is used synonymously with **grill.**

Knead: Working dough with your hands by repeatedly folding back, pressing forward, and turning the dough a quarter turn.

Marinade: A seasoned or flavored liquid, generally containing an acid (lemon juice, vinegar, or wine) with herbs and spices to flavor, and is sometimes used to tenderize meat, fish, or vegetables. The acid is necessary if the marinade is intended to tenderize the item, such as a tough cut of meat. Due to the acidic ingredients in most marinades, marinating should always be done in a glass, ceramic, stainless steel container, or a heavy-duty sealed plastic bag—never in aluminum to prevent the possibility of an unpleasant taste reaction.

Marinate: Soaking a food such as meat, fish, or vegetables in a seasoned liquid mixture called a **marinade** to enhance the food's flavoring or, in the instance of tough cuts of meat, to tenderize in preparation for cooking, roasting or grilling. In general, foods should be covered and refrigerated while marinating. When fruits are soaked in a flavored liquid (sugar syrup, liquor, liqueur, spices, etc.), the term used is **macerate**.

Melt: The process of using heat to convert a food item, such as butter, chocolate, or sugar, from a solid to a liquid or a semi-liquid.

Parboil: To partially cook food items by boiling for a short time and then plunging into an ice water bath to stop further cooking. This technique is used for firm foods such as carrots and potatoes so they can be added at the last minute to ingredients that cook faster. This technique may also be referred to as **blanching.**

Pare: To remove the thin outer layer of fruits and vegetables with a small, short-bladed knife, (generally referred to as a paring knife), or with a vegetable peeler.

Poach: Cooking in simmering liquid (heating the liquid until bubbles form slowly below the surface).

Purée: To process or mash food (usually a fruit or vegetable) until it is very smooth using a food processor, a blender, or by forcing/pressing the food through a fine sieve or food mill. The term also applies to the smooth-consistency food product that results from puréeing a fruit or vegetable in the manner just described.

Render: To place a fatty meat, such as bacon, in a pan over medium heat until the fat melts into the pan.

Roast: To cook food in the oven in an uncovered pan. The concept of the method is to expose the food to the heat of the oven, yielding a well-browned exterior and a moist interior. This method, therefore, requires tender cuts of meat and poultry because it is considered a dry-cooking method. This is not to be confused with the term **pot roast** which would be a moist-heat method of cooking cuts of meat that are not as tender, using a **braising** technique.

uté: Cooking food in an uncovered pan over direct, relatively high heat, stirring or tossing regularly until the food is cooked—or to a stage that is specified in the recipe. In general, the goal is not to brown the vegetables, but that can vary depending on the taste and character that is ideal for the end result of the recipe.

Scald:
- To heat a liquid, usually a dairy product, in the preparation of a yeast-bread, custard, pudding, or sauce recipe to just below the boiling point and until bubbles begin to break the surface—this would be approximately 180° to 185°F.

- To immerse vegetables or fruits (for example, tomatoes or peaches) into boiling water in order to loosen their skin to facilitate peeling. The produce item is left in the boiling water for 30 seconds and then plunged into an ice water bath to stop further cooking before the skin is removed. This technique may also be referred to as **blanching.**

Separating Eggs: When a recipe calls for only an egg white(s) or only an egg yolk(s), the egg's white must be separated from the yolk. Eggs are easiest to separate when cold, but whites reach their fullest volume when beaten if allowed to stand at room temperature for about 30 minutes before beating. Wash hands carefully after working with raw eggs. Below are methods to separate an egg.

- Many inexpensive egg separators are available at kitchen-supply stores. To separate, tap the midpoint of the egg sharply against a hard surface. Holding the egg over the egg separator that has been placed over a cup or small bowl, pull the shell halves apart gently. Let the yolk nestle into the cup-like center of the egg separator and the white will drop through the slots into the cup or bowl beneath. Drop 1 egg white at a time into the cup or small bowl and then transfer it to the mixing bowl before cracking another egg—this avoids the possibility of the yolk from the last egg getting into several whites. Drop the yolk into another mixing bowl if needed for the recipe, or into a storage container.

- Tap the midpoint of the egg sharply against a hard surface. Holding the egg over a cup or small bowl, pull the shell halves apart gently and lift the top part of the shell off the egg. Most of the white will run over the edge and into the cup/bowl below, while you cradle the yolk in the bottom half of the egg shell. Now, gently pour the yolk into the other half of the shell (or through your fingers), and more egg white will run out. Do this two or three times to pour off all of the egg white that clings around the yolk, and then dump the yolk into a separate bowl. Pour the egg white into the mixing bowl. Again, drop only one egg white at a time into the cup or small bowl and then transfer it to the mixing bowl.

Sift: To pass a dry ingredient or combination of dry ingredients through a fine strainer or flour sifter. Sifting removes large particles and lightens the ingredients by removing clumps and incorporating air while blending the ingredients to a certain degree.

Simmer: Heating a liquid (or cooking food in a liquid) that is just below the boiling point and until bubbles just begin to break the surface—this would be approximately 185°F (85°C) for watersimmering water in a pan.

Stir: Mixing ingredients around in a circular motion with a spoon or flexible spatula.

Truss: To wrap and tie chicken or meat securely with kitchen twine.

Whip: Beat rapidly to incorporate air into the ingredient(s). This technique is most often used for cream or egg whites to make them light and fluffy.

Adapted from cooking definitions by Catherine Pressler

INDEX

B

Baked Chicken Nuggets, 76
Baked Parmesan Zucchini, 39
baking,
Basic Cupcakes, 91
    Easy-to-Stuff Manicotti, 67
    Lasagna Cupcakes, 79
    Pigs in a Blanket, 82
    Quaker Oatmeal Prize-Winning
        Meatloaf, 71
    Quick Chili Mac, 81
    Tacos, 84
Berries
    Frozen Berry & Yogurt Pops, 87
    Peach Puffs, 90
    Strawberry Shortcake, 95 Very
        Berry Creme Caramel, 94
bitter taste,
Blackened Chicken, 61
boiling, 25
broiling, 26
Buffalo Wings, 78

C

Cheddar Mac & Cheese, 83
Cheesy Quesadillas, 69
chicken
    Baked Chicken Nuggets, 76
    Blackened Chicken, 61
    Buffalo Wings, 78
    Chicken and Rice Skillet, 56

    Chicken Marengo, 60
    Chicken Pita Sandwiches, 80
    Creamy Garlic Mushroom Chicken, 57
    Easy Kung Pao Chicken, 63
    Oven-Fried Chicken, 75
    Sheet-Pan Chicken Fajitas, 64
    Stir-Fried Chicken & Vegetables, 65
    Thai Chicken Stir-Fry, 59
Chicken and Rice Skillet, 56
Chicken Marengo, 60
Chicken Pita Sandwiches, 80
conversions, weights and measurements, 23
cooking methods, 25–26
cooking temperatures, 30
Cream Cheese Frosting, 92
Creamy Garlic Mushroom Chicken, 57
cuts, knife, 22

D

desserts
    Basic Cupcakes, 91
    Cream Cheese Frosting, 92
    Dark Chocolate Mousse, 89
    Frozen Berry & Yogurt Pops, 87
    Key Lime Cookies, 93
    Peach Puffs, 90
    Strawberry Shortcake, 95
    Tropical Carrot Cake, 86
    Vanilla Buttercream Frosting, 92
    Very Berry Creme Caramel, 94

E

Easy Kung Pao Chicken, 63
Easy-to-Stuff Manicotti, 67
entrees
    Baked Chicken Nuggets, 76
    Blackened Chicken, 61
    Buffalo Wings, 78
    Cheddar Mac & Cheese, 83
    Cheesy Quesadillas, 69
    Chicken and Rice Skillet, 56 Chicken
        Marengo, 60
    Chicken Pita Sandwiches, 80
    Creamy Garlic Mushroom Chicken, 57
    Easy Kung Pao Chicken, 63
    Easy-to-Stuff Manicotti, 67
    Fettuccine Primavera, 68
    Homemade Pizza, 72-74
    Lasagna Cupcakes, 79
    Oven-Fried Chicken, 75
    Pigs in a Blanket, 82
    Quaker Oatmeal Prize-Winning
        Meatloaf, 71
    Quick Chili Mac, 81
    Sheet-Pan Chicken Fajitas, 64
    Steamed Jasmine Rice, 66
    Stir-Fried Chicken & Vegetables, 65
    Tacos, 84
    Thai Chicken Stir-Fry, 59
Equipment list, kitchen, 12

F

Fettuccine Primavera, 68
food safety, 29
fruit desserts
    Frozen Berry & Yogurt Pops, 87
    Key Lime Cookies, 93
    Peach Puffs, 90
    Strawberry Shortcake, 95
    Tropical Carrot Cake, 86
    Very Berry Creme Caramel, 94

H

herbs, 27
Homemade Pizza, 72-74
Honey-Glazed Baby Carrots, 44

K

Key Lime Cookies, 93
kitchen equipment, 11
knife skills, safety, 21

L

Lasagna Cupcakes, 79

M

Mashed Yukon Potatoes, 49
measuring, 33
Mesclun Spring Mix Salad with Balsamic
Vinaigrette, 43
methods, cooking, 25–26

O

Oven-Fried Chicken, 75

P

pasta
    Cheddar Mac & Cheese, 83
    Easy-to-Stuff Manicotti, 67
    Fettuccine Primavera, 68
    Lasagna Cupcakes, 79
    Quick Chili Mac, 81
Peach Puffs, 90
Pigs in a Blanket, 82
Pizza, homemade, 72-74
poaching, 25
potatoes
    Mashed Yukon Potatoes, 49
    Pommes Anna, 48
    Potato Pancakes, 47
    Scalloped Potatoes, 52
    Seasoned Baked Potato Wedges, 50
    varieties, 46

Q

Quaker Oatmeal Prize-Winning Meatloaf, 71
Quick Chili Mac, 81

R

Ratatouille, 41
recipe reading, 31
resting, 26
rice
  Chicken and Rice Skillet, 56
  Steamed Jasmine Rice, 66
Roasted Green Beans with Parmesan &
Basil, 38 roasting, 25

S

safety
  food, 29
  knife, 23
Salad, Mesclun Spring Mix with Balsamic
  Vinaigrette, 43
salty taste, 17
sautéing, 26
savory taste, 17
Scalloped Potatoes, 52
searing, 26
Seasoned Baked Potato Wedges, 50
Sheet-Pan Chicken Fajitas, 64
simmering, 25
Sour taste, 17
spices, 27
Steamed Jasmine Rice, 66
Stir-Fried Chicken & Vegetables, 65
Strawberry Shortcake, 95
supplies, kitchen, 11
sweet taste, 17

T

Tacos, 84
tastes, five basic 17
temperature, 30
Thai Chicken Stir-Fry, 59
Tropical Carrot Cake, 86

U

umami taste, 17

V

Vanilla Buttercream Frosting, 92
vegetables
  Baked Parmesan Zucchini, 39
  Fettuccine Primavera, 68
  Honey-Glazed Baby Carrots, 44
  *Mesclun Spring Mix Salad with
    Balsamic Vinaigrette, 43*
  Ratatouille, 41
  *Roasted Green Beans with Parmesan
    & Basil, 38*
  Stir-Fried Chicken & Vegetables, 65
Very Berry Creme Caramel, 94

W

weights and measurements, 3

CPSIA information can be obtained
at www.ICGtesting.com
Printed in the USA
BVHW020947040921
615902BV00030B/623